Mendips

Woolton, Liverpool

THE NATIONAL TRUST

DREAMING IN MENDIPS

BY YOKO ONO LENNON

LIVERPOOL meant a great deal to John. He was always talking about Liverpool, his home town. It all started in Mendips, his childhood home. Whenever I came up to Liverpool with him, we would drive along Menlove Avenue, and he would point at the house and say, 'Yoko, look, look. That's it!' By then, his Aunt Mimi, who brought him up here, had moved away, and we couldn't get to see the inside. But the way John was describing the place to me, I felt like I knew every room: the kitchen, where John and Uncle George sat together and spoke in low voices of the feelings they shared; the back yard, where the student lodgers used to tell John about the world; and the upstairs bedroom, where John used to write down things in his diary in gobblygook, so Mimi would not understand them, even if she were to read them. And what about the staircase and the upstairs landing which he tried not to let creak, when he came back home late?!

When I heard that Mendips was up for sale, I was worried that it might fall into the wrong hands and be commercially exploited. That's why I decided to buy the house, and donate it to the National Trust so it would be well looked after as a place for people to visit and see. I am thrilled that the National Trust has agreed to take it on. Now everyone who loves John's music and his message of peace can see for themselves where it all began.

Everything that happened afterwards germinated from John's dreaming in his little bedroom at Mendips, which was a very special place for him. John's public face was that of an extrovert, but, privately, John was a quiet, sensitive introvert who was always dreaming of what he wanted in life. An incredible dreamer, John made those dreams come true – for himself and for the world.

Walking into that room today, so many years later, still gives me goosebumps. I hope you'll make your dream come true, too, as John did his.

Above John and his cousin Michael standing in the front porch before it was enclosed in 1952

Left John and Yoko in January 1970

Love,
Yoko Ono Lennon

3

There's a place where I can go

THE HOUSE

'I lived in the suburbs in a nice semi-detached place with a small garden and doctors and lawyers and that ilk living around … I was a nice clean-cut suburban boy.' JOHN LENNON

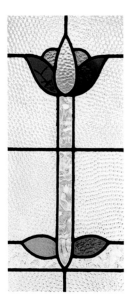

Mendips was built in 1933 as a three-bedroom semi-detached house near the corner of Vale Road and Menlove Avenue in the Liverpool suburb of Woolton. The builders who put up the house offered potential buyers a choice of stylistic trimmings, to give the new development a sense of variety: you could have Art Nouveau stained glass, Olde English half-timbering or perhaps an Art Deco fireplace. But beneath the skin, the basic skeleton did not change: on the ground floor, the staircase/entrance hall runs alongside a front lounge, leading to a morning room, dining room and kitchen. Upstairs, there are two large and one small bedrooms, grouped round a central stairwell, with a bathroom and separate toilet at the back. Alongside and behind the house is a good-sized private garden.

Thousands and thousands of houses just like Mendips were built on the outskirts of Britain's towns and cities in the 1930s, creating the suburbia we know today. Their mishmash style was mocked as 'By-pass Variegated' by the architectural critic Osbert Lancaster, writing in 1938. He criticised the suburban semi as badly planned, and predicted that it would become the slum of the future. Contrary to Mr Lancaster's predictions, these houses have proved remarkably well suited to the changing needs of British family life, and have been looked after by those who have lived in them.

From the 1930s onwards, it was the dream of most working- and lower-middle-class families to live in a house like Mendips. The name itself had allure, evoking the classic rolling English countryside of north-east Somerset. Mendips is less than a mile away from 20 Forthlin Road, where Paul McCartney was brought up, but, socially, it was a different world. Forthlin Road had a number; Mendips had a name. They shared a similar layout, but Mendips had those all-important bay windows that offered extra space and status. The bellboard you can still see in the Morning Room at Mendips suggests that the owners were expected to employ a maid and to call the front room 'the drawing room', although in fact John's family did neither, but Paul remembers Mendips as 'one of the almost posh houses in the posh area'.

It was in this unlikely setting that one of the 20th century's most creative and influential rebels grew up.

Above The Art Nouveau-style stained glass

Top right One of the original light switches

Right 'By-pass Variegated'. Osbert Lancaster's vision of 1930s suburbia

Left John by the front gate in the early 1950s

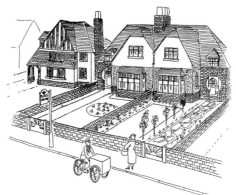

A house where there is love

LIVING WITH AUNT MIMI

'I'd say I had a happy childhood. I came out aggressive, but I was never miserable. I was always having a laugh.' JOHN LENNON

John Winston Lennon was born on 9 October 1940 in Oxford Street maternity hospital, Liverpool. His parents were Fred Lennon, a merchant seaman, and Julia Stanley, one of five sisters, who were to be the dominant influence on John's early life. Fred's long periods away at sea put a growing strain on the marriage, which finally dissolved in 1942. Later on, Julia moved from Newcastle Road into a flat in nearby Gateacre with her new boyfriend John Dykins. In 1945, when John was five, he came to live at Mendips with Julia's sister, Mary (always known as Mimi), and her husband George Smith, who had no children of their own.

Aunt Mimi was a tall, no-nonsense woman who believed in discipline and kept Mendips immaculately tidy; Uncle George was much softer-hearted. Together, they provided the stable and loving home that John badly needed. George taught John to read by sitting him on a knee and picking out words in the *Liverpool Echo* syllable by syllable. Newspaper headlines were always to be an important inspiration for John's lyrics. There were plenty of books in the house, and John soon became a voracious reader. Particular early favourites were Richmal Crompton's *Just William* books, which probably fuelled his rebellious streak, and *Alice in Wonderland*. Lewis Carroll's fantasy world may have influenced songs such as 'I am the Walrus' and John's books such as *John Lennon in His Own Write*. John's other passions were painting and drawing, and listening

to the radio: he loved mimicking the nonsense voices on *The Goon Show*.

In 1945 John started going to Dovedale primary school, taking the bus every day to Penny Lane past Strawberry Field. At school, he stood out at once: his first headmaster thought him 'as sharp as a needle'. He was always the centre of attention and of trouble, objecting especially at having to wear school uniform. Despite this, John, who showed an exceptional talent for art, sailed easily through his eleven-plus exam.

Above John in the garden at Mendips in the early 1950s

Right John with his uncle, George Smith, and Sally the dog in the early 1950s

John remembered his childhood as a generally happy time, but, although his mother was a frequent visitor to Mendips, the sadness of absent parents remained. In July 1946 Fred Lennon reappeared without warning on the doorstep to reclaim his son. He took John away to Blackpool, where Julia eventually caught up with them. At the age of only five, John was given the ghastly task of choosing between his parents. After a tearful hesitation, he agreed to return to live at Mendips, but this heart-rending episode left scars.

Left John with his Aunt Mimi in the early 1950s

You can't do that

TEENAGE REBEL

In September 1952 John started at Quarry Bank
High School. He found the traditional grammar
school atmosphere there oppressive and reacted
to it with bouts of skiving, smoking and swearing.
He whiled away the lessons sketching acid caricatures of his teachers in an exercise book known as
the *Daily Howl*. With increasing desperation, Aunt
Mimi devoted her time and energy to getting him
back on the straight and narrow: 'He never came
home to an empty house', she remembered. This
became all the more difficult after her husband
died suddenly in 1955 – the second great shock
in John's life after his parents' separation.

In 1956 John heard Elvis Presley's 'Heartbreak
Hotel' on Radio Luxembourg for the first time.
'After that, nothing was the same for me'. He
stuck up a poster of Elvis in his bedroom, which
became a total mess, despite his aunt's strictures.
His other great hero at that time was Lonnie
Donegan, creator of skiffle, the homemade
English version of American rock 'n' roll. He
would play a 78 of Donegan's 'Rock Island Line'
over and over again on his mother's old record
player until the disc was worn out.

John's next step was to buy himself a guitar,
which he smuggled into the house by claiming
that his mother had given it to him; in fact, it cost
him £5 10s by mail order. Ambitious to improve,
he badgered Julia into getting a rather better,
Spanish-style model. His fingers were soon raw

Right John (middle row) in May 1957, two months before he first met Paul McCartney. From the Quarry Bank school photo

Above right A self-portrait of John from *John Lennon in His Own Write*. He began drawing caricatures as a bored schoolboy

awkward. As Paul plays left-handed, the necks of their guitars tended to collide. Mimi disapproved of the noise and would often banish them to the porch. It was easier to cycle over to Forthlin Road and practise there, while Paul's father was out.

John left Quarry Bank school without regret or qualifications, but in later life he took a perverse pride in wearing his old school tie. His talent for art and a recommendation from his headmaster were enough to get him a place at Liverpool College of Art, where he started in the autumn of 1957. Although already ambitious, John showed more interest in music and girls than in his studies. Mimi despaired, but John's mother was supportive. Since the death of Uncle George, John had become closer to Julia, who was living at 1 Blomfield Road in nearby Allerton. She was a red-haired, fun-loving free spirit, who had taught him how to play the banjo and now encouraged the rebel in him. John's friend Pete Shotton remembered, 'She did everything for laughs, just like us.'

On 15 July 1958, Julia had come for tea and a chat with her sister at Mendips. As she was crossing the road outside the house to catch a bus home, she was knocked down and killed by a car driven by an off-duty policeman. She was only 44. Though he did not show it at first, the tragedy affected John deeply, making him increasingly bitter at the world. His feelings only emerged years later, when he wrote 'Julia' and other songs in her memory. It also strengthened the bond with Paul, whose mother had died young the previous year.

John's childhood was over.

red with practising chords. Armed with this, he formed his own amateur skiffle group, the Quarry Men, which played at many local venues. On 6 July 1957 the group was performing at St Peter's church fête in Woolton, when he first met the fifteen-year-old Paul McCartney. John was not easily impressed, but here was someone who could really tune and play a guitar, and knew all the chords to his favourite Little Richard and Gene Vincent songs. John asked him to join the group, and the partnership at the heart of the Beatles was forged.

When Paul started coming round to Mendips, Mimi warmed to his good manners: 'John, your little friend's here,' she would call up to him. John and Paul would sit for hours on his bed in the upstairs front room, picking out tunes, and beginning to compose their own songs. 'Please Please Me', 'I Call Your Name' and 'I'll Get You' all began life at Mendips. But it was

Imagine

AFTERWARDS

Over the next three years, John and Paul's band went through numerous changes of name and personnel as it gradually refined its own style of rock 'n' roll in the clubs of Liverpool and Hamburg. John was away from Mendips for much of this time, as his band, now called the Beatles, went from being local Liverpool celebrities to a national phenomenon. But Mendips remained his home, and for a time that of his first wife, Cynthia, and their son Julian, to which he would make flying visits.

Even after the worldwide success of the Beatles, Mimi tried to carry on as normal at Mendips. She took pity on the fans who had trekked hundreds of miles for a sight of John's childhood home, inviting them in for tea and sandwiches. But she found that she had to start locking the kitchen door to stop them pinching crockery as souvenirs.

Mimi was unchanged by John's sudden and enormous fame. She was proud of her nephew's achievements, but never sought to exploit the connection. To her, John always remained the wayward, but essentially soft-hearted teenager in need of firm guidance. When she decided in 1965 to retire to Poole in Dorset, John bought her a bungalow there. John himself would have liked to hang on to Mendips ('Mimi, I grew up there. Let's keep it'), but she wanted to sell, and so they did.

Above Aunt Mimi in the Lounge at Mendips. A photo of John sits proudly on top of the TV

Right The Fab Four photographed in 1963 at the height of Beatlemania

After the breakup of the Beatles, John settled in New York with his wife Yoko and their son Sean. He did not return to Mendips, but he never forgot his years there.

Left John performing in the Cavern Club in Liverpool in December 1961

THE PORCH

Aunt Mimi refused to let John and Paul practise in the house, and so they often took refuge here. They were unlikely to be interrupted, as the front door was rarely used. They found that the hard surfaces of the bare walls and the glass panels generated just the right boomy, 'bathroom' acoustic they wanted for their sound. Here John would play for hours by himself on the guitar Mimi had bought him for £17 from Hessy's music store in Liverpool.

The Art Nouveau-style glass and the leaded lights were designed to give the house an extra cachet.

Right The porch was enclosed in 1952

When I get home

TOUR OF THE HOUSE

The Kitchen
Most visitors came into the house through the back door via the Kitchen.

Here Mimi would cook John his favourite meal – egg and chips, washed down with a cup of tea. Here also she proudly hung a framed copy of John's poem, 'A house where there is love'.

Mimi modernised the Kitchen in the 1960s with a yellow formica worktop and a double-drainer sink, which stood facing the window to the garden. The floor was covered with black and white kitchen tiles. The Kitchen has been refitted several times since, like kitchens everywhere, but the National Trust has replicated most of the 1950s features.

The Morning Room
This was the heart of the house. John ate his meals in this cosy room at a drop-leaf table pulled out from the wall. Mimi would sit here doing running repairs at her Singer sewing machine. There were also a radio on the window sill and an antique grandfather clock inscribed 'George Toogood, Woolton Tavern', which had come down in George's family.

The Dining Room
This room had many different uses over the years. It was the family dining room, but student lodgers also used it as their sitting room and study.

The Lounge
The built-in bookshelves were put up in the 1950s, but the Tudor-arched, tiled fireplace was apparently moved here from the Dining Room

Above The electric bellboard in the Morning Room was meant to summon servants, although John's family had none

Right The Lounge in the early 1960s. The built-in book shelves survive, but the Art Deco open fireplace has been removed

after John left, replacing a more Art Deco-style open fire.

John would sit in this room writing poetry and song lyrics: 'He never had a pencil out of his hand', Mimi remembered, 'He'd write something down, then screw up the bit of paper and throw it away and start again. And he'd say: "You ought to pick these up, Mimi, because I'm going to be famous one day and they'll be worth something."'

The Hall
John recalled that the far end of the Hall was hung with a watercolour of a Chinese vase painted by his Uncle George. Mimi displayed some of her good collection of Coalport, Spode and Crown Derby porcelain on the plate rack here.

John's Room

As a young boy, John would be sent off to bed with his panda under one arm and his teddy under the other. Mimi remembered him singing himself to sleep. He would sit for hours here, drawing with his pencils and crayons, or listening to the wireless on an extension speaker from the family radio in the Morning Room downstairs.

John belonged to the first generation of post-war teenagers, who pioneered the teenage bedroom. When the rock 'n' roll craze struck in the mid-50s, John's room became a total turmoil and out of bounds to Mimi: 'Leave it, I'll tidy it up'. But he never did. Posters of Elvis, Rita Hayworth and Brigitte Bardot covered the walls and ceiling.

Here John would talk about the latest American rock 'n' roll records with Paul, and here he began the extraordinary collaboration that became the most famous partnership in the history of pop music. As Yoko recalls, 'Everything that happened afterwards germinated from John's dreaming in his little bedroom.'

The Front Bedroom

This was the main bedroom at Mendips, where Mimi and George slept.

The Bathroom

This has retained some of its 1930s fittings, including the wall tiles, mirrored cabinet and airing cupboard.

Above The bathroom retains its original tiles and glass holder

Right John covered his bedroom walls with posters of Brigitte Bardot, whose *Et Dieu …Crea la Femme (And God created Woman)* was released in Britain in 1956

The Back Bedroom is not open to visitors, as it is being used by the custodian. In John's day, it was the spare bedroom, often occupied by student lodgers.

The Garden

In John's time, the back garden was more open, and the shrubs were smaller. Both Mimi and George were keen gardeners, and they kept the garden as neat and tidy as the inside of the house. They were particularly fond of soft fruit, such as gooseberries, blackberries, redcurrants and raspberries, which they grew on the left-hand side of the garden.

John earned his five shillings pocket money by pushing the mower around the garden after he came home from school. He did the job quickly and badly!

Above An Art Deco-style fireplace in the main bedroom

Left John's bike leans against the outside wall of the Morning Room in the early 1950s

15